Green

poetry by

Theresa Senato Edwards

Finishing Line Press
Georgetown, Kentucky

Green

Copyright © 2016 by Theresa Senato Edwards
ISBN 978-1-944899-19-6 First Edition
All rights reserved under International and Pan-American Copyright Conventions.
No part of this book may be reproduced in any manner whatsoever without written permission from the publisher, except in the case of brief quotations embodied in critical articles and reviews.

ACKNOWLEDGMENTS

Green, first published by Another New Calligraphy, March 2015

Thanks to Dr. Jane Wohl and one of her writing workshops years ago at Goddard College, for helping me realize this story, one I had no idea I wanted to tell.

A special thanks to Leah Maines for accepting this book not once but twice. This republished edition would not have been possible without her.

Thanks always to my family and friends.

Cover artist Frank Valvano's artwork collection includes commercial arts, drawing, painting, sculpture, and graphic design. His work has been featured in local art shows, coffee shops, and businesses near his home in Westchester County, New York. Valvano has successfully sold many of his abstract landscape paintings, his specialty. For more information about his art, please contact vansworld2000@aol.com.

Editor: Christen Kincaid

Cover Art: Frank Valvano

Author Photo: Douglas Edwards

Cover Design: Elizabeth Maines

Printed in the USA on acid-free paper.
Order online: www.finishinglinepress.com
       also available on amazon.com

Author inquiries and mail orders:
Finishing Line Press
P. O. Box 1626
Georgetown, Kentucky 40324
U. S. A.

Grandson: I don't like walking around this
old and empty house.

MM: Just a little green,
It's the house telling you to close your eyes.

Grandson: Wait, wait, wait for me, please hang around.
I'll see you when I fall asleep.

MM: Just a little green,
have a happy ending.

~

Sources: Of Monsters and Men, "Little Talks"
Joni Mitchell, "Little Green"

I

He never knew his grandfather,
never saw the gray of his skin.

But his grandmother—
Mary Miglio, MM for short

he knew her walk,
her voice, the smell of her home:
a mix of dying lilacs left
in water too long.

He found honeysuckle
under her bed pillows,
five years of garden magazines
lined her front bedroom.

Green vats on windowsills.

The slope of the valley
in each particle of glass.

He reflected,   smell of rose
when MM pruned each stem,
blue / green garden gloves,

blood spots seeping through
the indexes.

Mist creeped
along the edge of his memory:

*MM lived her whole life in the house,
greens and blues.*

Something green
attached to his arm,
sucked his skin raw
before he pulled it off,
flicked it into the thick smell of dead flowers.

green
pond near evergreens—
grandmother's shadow:
   what happens to some joined
to loss,
        the turning   not many see

~

he put pressure on the wound.

II

Her grandchildren never noticed time—
transient in the frame of grandmother's home,
evenings of peach ice cream.

Lightning in the ground:

sparks from grass when
he ran from his parents' car
to the front door, slight halos
around each daffodil lining
the steps.

Smell of blue
on her front porch.
    The longing stopped:
MM lightening—
her grandson's heaviness
    quiet on the overhang.

III

When MM was 82, she bought
a trampoline for the backyard
for great grandchildren (none yet his)

14 feet diameter, blue plastic safety pad
around the circumference.

She covered it,
green knit blanket.

On certain nights,
it collected
beneath soft fibers—   sounds
on the far edge of breath,

grandson's dreams
     on the back bedroom window (eyes
        lock,   his hands slowly sift
sienna curls   love's cheekbones,
  smooth pressing).

Once or twice, the smell of pond lifted
with wind,

   something extreme settled
   in MM's home:
   green,   a solitary pause—

*MM lived her whole life in the house,
greens and blues.*

IV

On days when she rode her bike six miles
to / from town,

MM ate a raw onion sandwich.
Like an old cowboy, she'd say.

Pin the bad-breath lapel on me,
strap me to the saddle.

Eating raw onions warmed MM's toes.

Barefoot
she mounted the black of trampoline,
gave in to the stretch and pull of lithe,
strong strands.

Spring afternoon
against clear sky.
MM's back garden crisp—

new growth, crocuses already into their
late-day stretch.

Spring in MM's body—

On the periphery,
cat eyes followed air as it threw her up
and over the smooth edge of life.

MM's vats collecting,
        each row,   dampened years
house emptying
   (a root cellar under the kitchen).

V

Mist rose a half inch
from her bedroom floor.

Something green left
a small valley on MM's grandson.
Grandmother's desk frame sharp
against his head.

Smell of blue helped his mind close.

    Pond air rearranging
    sleep collecting
        like gifts

daffodils
        a narrative: subtle finding—
        slope of chin,
        love's collar bone delicately

    waiting
grandson weightless —

MM gathered lilacs,
    her home participating.

Time yielded to her grandson's settling.

Home yielded / settled—easing   its way

~

blue.

Theresa Senato Edwards' work includes two full-length poetry books: *Voices Through Skin*, (Sibling Rivalry Press) and *Painting Czeslawa Kwoka ~ Honoring Children of the Holocaust*, full-color collaboration with Painter, Lori Schreiner (unbound CONTENT); the latter won a Tacenda Literary Award for Best Book. Other work: two poetry chapbooks, *Green* (first published in a different format by Another New Calligraphy), which includes an instrumental cd with the poet's digital reinterpretation of the second movement of her Piano Sonata #1, Pauline Lederer, pianist, and *The Music of Hands* (Webbook, Seven CirclePress; first print edition, self published). Excerpts from Edwards' manuscript in progress entitled, "Wing Bones," can be found in *Gargoyle* and online at *The Nervous Breakdown*. Edwards was nominated for a Pushcart Prize in 2012 and received a writing residency from Drop Forge & Tool in 2015. Her blog: www.tsenatoedwards.blogspot.com.

www.ingramcontent.com/pod-product-compliance
Lightning Source LLC
Chambersburg PA
CBHW060227050426
42446CB00013B/3207